COLUMBUS
** DAY **

WITHDRAWN

Joanna Ponto

Enslow Publishing
101 W. 23rd Street
Suite 240
New York, NY 10011
USA

enslow.com

Published in 2017 by Enslow Publishing, LLC.
101 W. 23rd Street, Suite 240, New York, NY 10011

Library of Congress Cataloging-in-Publication Data
Names: Ponto, Joanna, author.
Title: Columbus Day / Joanna Ponto.
Description: New York, NY : Enslow Publishing, 2017. | Series: The story of our holidays | Includes
   bibliographical references and index. | Audience: Ages 8-up. | Audience: Grade 4 to 6.
Identifiers: LCCN 2016001028| ISBN 9780766076570 (library bound) | ISBN 9780766076549 (pbk.) |
   ISBN 9780766076563 (6-pack)
Subjects: LCSH: Columbus Day--Juvenile literature. | Columbus, Christopher--Juvenile literature. |
   America--Discovery and exploration--Spanish--Juvenile literature.
Classification: LCC E120 .P77 2016 | DDC 394.264--dc23
LC record available at http://lccn.loc.gov/2016001028

Printed in the United States of America

To Our Readers: We have done our best to make sure all websites in this book were active and appropriate when we went to press. However, the author and the publisher have no control over and assume no liability for the material available on those websites or on any websites they may link to. Any comments or suggestions can be sent by e-mail to customerservice@enslow.com.

Portions of this book originally appeared in the book *Columbus Day: Celebrating a Famous Explorer* by Elaine Landau.

Contents

Chapter 1

A Day to Celebrate Columbus 5

Chapter 2

The Man Behind the Holiday 8

Chapter 3

Setting Sail 13

Chapter 4

A Whole New World 17

Chapter 5

The Start of Columbus Day 21

Chapter 6

How Do You Celebrate? 25

Columbus Day Craft. 28

Glossary 30

Learn More 31

Index. 32

Many cities and towns across the United States hold parades to celebrate Columbus Day. This float features a likeness of Christopher Columbus at the wheel of a ship.

Chapter 1

A Day to Celebrate Columbus

Columbus Day is a holiday when we celebrate the accomplishments of Christopher Columbus. Hundreds of years ago, this man from Genoa, Italy, dreamed of sailing to an unknown place.

To the New World

Columbus is famous for crossing the Atlantic Ocean by ship to reach the Americas. This was a whole new world that people in Europe did not know about. But Columbus had not really hoped to find that part of the world. When he left Europe, he was looking for a way to get to Asia by sea. There were many new and exciting things in Asia. Columbus hoped to bring back some of them when he returned home.

Upon landing in the West Indies, Columbus made claim to the New World.

Instead of reaching Asia, Columbus landed on an island in the Caribbean Sea that is now one of the islands of the West Indies. Columbus traveled to the New World four times between 1492 and 1504 to explore the West Indies. He also explored the coasts of Central America and South America.

Columbus's Contribution

Some people think that Columbus discovered America, but this is not quite true. The American Indians living there had arrived many years earlier. Columbus was not even the first European to sail there. In about AD 1000, Viking adventurers, from the area that is now Denmark, Norway, and Sweden landed on the coast of North America. But they did not stay very long.

Columbus's trips led to a lasting link between Europe and the Americas. In time, other explorers followed, and trade and colonies grew. Christopher Columbus earned a place in history.

We remember Christopher Columbus each year on the second Monday in October because Columbus landed in the West Indies on October 12, 1492.

Chapter 2

The Man Behind the Holiday

In 1451, in a busy Italian seaport called Genoa, Christoforo Colombo was born. We know him as Christopher Columbus. We do not know much about Columbus's childhood, but we do know he had four brothers and sisters. He was close to his brothers Bartholomew and Diego. They played together when they were children. As adults, they often worked together.

Columbus worked for a trader. Traders traveled to distant lands, where they bought and sold many different things. By the 1470s, Columbus had gone on several trading trips. He went to France in Europe, Tunisia in Africa, and other countries. He learned about trading and sailing.

On to Portugal

Columbus moved from Italy to Portugal in 1476. Columbus's brother Bartholomew was in Portugal. The two brothers designed and sold maps to traders. They lived in Lisbon, a very busy seaport.

In 1479, Christopher married a young woman named Felipa Perestrello de Moñiz. A year later they had a son, Diego. Felipa's father was governor of Porto Santo, a Portuguese island off the coast of northern Africa. Columbus lived there with his wife and child for a while.

Columbus the Businessman?

No one really ever thought that Christopher Columbus would someday become a famous explorer. His father and grandfather were wool weavers. But his father hoped that his eldest son would someday become a very important businessman.

A Route to Asia

In the early 1480s, Columbus sailed to the Canary Islands, a group of islands off the Western coast of Africa. He also visited West Africa, where he learned about the trade in slaves, gold, and diamonds.

Columbus knew that what European traders needed most was a safe and shorter route to Asia. Gold, silk, and spices could be found there. Spices were not only put in food. They were also used as medicines, and people paid a lot of money for them.

But Asia was extremely hard to get to. It was a long and costly trip by land. Sailors reached Asia in a roundabout way. They sailed south and then east around Africa. The passage was difficult and dangerous. Many ships were wrecked in storms at sea. Pirates sometimes attacked these vessels.

Columbus studied all his maps and charts. Finally he came up with a new route to Asia. He wanted to sail west rather than east.

Trade was an important part of the economies of Spain and Portugal. Columbus wanted to be a part of it.

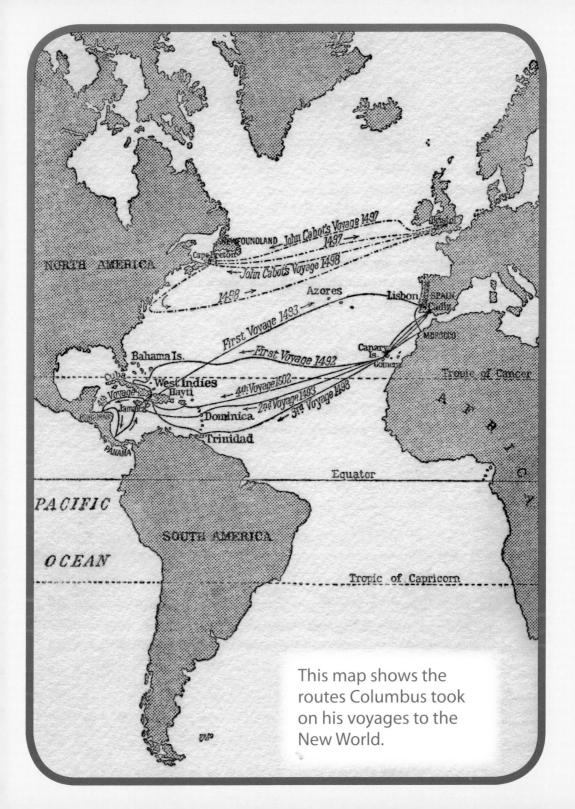

This map shows the routes Columbus took on his voyages to the New World.

Columbus thought this would shorten the trip. After all, the earth is round, so sailors should be able to get to Asia from either direction.

A Few Mistakes

Columbus thought the world was smaller than it was. That made him sure that Asia was closer to Europe than it really was. There were other problems with Columbus's plan. The earth is mostly covered with water. But Columbus's maps showed it was covered with mostly land. He believed that Asia stretched farther east than it does.

Columbus also thought sailing west was the best way to go. That was wrong, too. Two large bodies of land blocked his path. Those areas of land were North and South America. Columbus did not know anything about these continents.

Christopher Columbus wished to try out his new route. But he needed people to help pay for the costly voyage. He had to have at least three ships to carry enough food, water, and supplies for a long trip. First, he had to make others believe that he was right.

Today we know that Columbus never reached Asia. Instead, he found something far more valuable.

Chapter 3

Setting Sail

Ready to put his theories to the test, Columbus met with King John II of Portugal in 1483. Columbus hoped the king would help pay for his voyage. But the king turned Columbus down. Columbus refused to give up.

The years ahead were difficult for Columbus. Many people laughed at his ideas. His wife died sometime between 1484 and 1485. Discouraged, Columbus left Portugal with his son, Diego, and went to Spain.

Encouragement From Spain

In 1486, Columbus went before King Ferdinand and Queen Isabella of Spain. He asked them if they would help pay for his voyage to Asia. The queen liked Columbus. She also liked the idea of finding a faster way to get to Asia. Yet, her advisers told her it was impossible. Queen Isabella was not quite convinced that Columbus was wrong, however. The royal treasurer, Luís de Santangel, also thought Columbus might be right. At the time, Spain did not have enough money to help pay for Columbus's voyage.

Columbus appealed to Spain's King Ferdinand and Queen Isabella to fund his voyage.

Finally, a Chance

Then in the spring of 1492 things changed. Spain had won a war. Now it had money for Columbus's voyage. Luís de Santangel urged the queen to help pay for Columbus's voyage, and she listened.

Columbus had three ships—the *Niña*, the *Pinta,* and the *Santa María*. Columbus was captain of the *Santa María*, the largest ship. Back then, ships did not have engines. The crew had to move the ships using ropes and sails. Only the officers had sleeping quarters. The sailors found places to sleep on the open deck. In bad weather they slept down below. The men ate salty meat or fish and hard biscuits. They drank wine mixed with water.

The Voyage

On August 3, 1492, Columbus's three ships left Palos, Spain. The first stop was the Canary Islands, where the ships would be stocked with fresh food, water, and wood. At first the crew felt lucky. The winds were strong and in their favor. The ships made good time. But after about a month things changed. The men wondered why they had not reached land yet.

Fear spread among the men on the three ships. All had heard stories about sea monsters and now wondered if they could be true. Many felt they would never reach Asia.

Land was finally spotted on October 12, 1492. Columbus was sure he was in Asia. He could not have been more wrong.

Columbus and his crew set sail on the *Niña*, the *Pinta*, and the *Santa María* in August 1492.

Chapter 4

A Whole New World

Columbus had sailed to the West Indies instead. These islands are just southeast of Florida on the east coast of the United States.

Columbus and the Indians

The native people on the islands lived in peaceful villages. They farmed and wove cloth. Columbus called the native people Indians because he thought he was in the East Indies.

The Indians gave Columbus and his men food and shelter. But their kindness was not returned. In time, Columbus and his men made the Indians work long hours and gave them little food. If the Indians disobeyed, they were harshly punished. Many died from the lack of food and the cruel treatment they received.

Columbus presented gifts to the islands' native people. Believing he was in Asia, he called them Indians.

Some Indians died of diseases the Europeans brought with them. Columbus had also brought Christianity to the Indians. He thought that this made up for what the Indians lost, but he was wrong.

Continued Travels

Columbus left some of his men on the island and set sail with the others to explore. His next stop was the northern coast of the island of Hispaniola. Columbus took control of it and claimed it for Spain. He also traveled to Cuba. He thought it might be Japan. In Cuba he found a small amount of gold and a new grain called corn. (Try making cornmeal griddle cakes using the recipe on page 20 to get an idea of what Columbus might have eaten.)

Columbus continued his travels. He hoped to find China before returning to Spain, but the *Santa María* was wrecked on a reef near Haiti. Once again the native people on the island helped Columbus. He left about forty of his men in Haiti to build a fort and search for gold.

Returning a Hero

The *Niña* and *Pinta* headed for Spain. The trip was extremely difficult. Some of the Indians Columbus had brought along died. And there were terrible storms at sea.

When he got to Spain, Columbus was treated like a hero. King Ferdinand and Queen Isabella ordered a second voyage to the New World. In all, Columbus made four trips there. He explored the islands of Puerto Rico, Trinidad, and Jamaica. He explored parts of Central America and South America as well.

Columbus never found the riches he dreamed of. He also had many disappointments and suffered many hardships before dying in 1506. By then, he knew there was no quick route to Asia. But he never realized one important thing: He had opened the door to a whole new world.

Cornmeal Griddle Cakes*

Ingredients:

½ cup (80 grams) cornmeal
2 tablespoons (30 g) corn oil
   or melted butter
½ cup (60 g) all-purpose flour
¼ cup (17 g) powdered milk
1 teaspoon (5 g) baking
   powder
1 cup (240 mL) water

Directions:

1. Mix the cornmeal, flour, powdered milk, and baking powder together with a spatula or wooden spoon in a large bowl.
2. Mix the water and oil (or melted butter) together.
3. Beat the water and oil (or butter) into the dry ingredients with a whisk.
4. Heat a griddle or cast-iron pan on the stove on medium-high heat. Add a little oil or butter.
5. Drop spoonfuls of the batter onto the hot pan or griddle. When the first side is golden brown, turn the cake over and brown the other side.

* Adult supervision required.

Chapter 5

The Start of Columbus Day

Even though we give Columbus credit for "finding" the New World, the area was not named for him. North and South America were named for another Italian explorer named Amerigo Vespucci.

Remembering Columbus

Christopher Columbus was not forgotten, however. The country Colombia was named for him. So were the District of Columbia, Columbus, Ohio, and Columbus, Georgia. Many other cities, streets, schools, and buildings in the United States have Columbus's name.

There are also statues and monuments to honor Christopher Columbus. Paintings of him hang in many buildings. Often museums and libraries have exhibits about Columbus. Some trace his route to the Americas.

The first official Columbus Day celebration was held on October 12, 1792. That was the three hundredth anniversary of Columbus's landing. A group known as the Society of St. Tammany, or the Colombian Order, planned it. The idea did not catch on right away. There were only small celebrations in different parts of the country. Often Italian-American groups sponsored these gatherings.

Columbus Day Parades

The next large Columbus Day celebration was in 1892, the four hundredth anniversary of Columbus's arrival. President Benjamin Harrison asked Americans everywhere to celebrate. Schools put on shows about Columbus. Community centers had parties and dances. A ballet called *Columbus and the Discovery of America* was written.

After 1892, Columbus Day was celebrated more regularly. In 1909, New York became the first state to declare it an official holiday. On October 12 the governor led a grand parade. Many states also made Columbus Day a legal holiday. Usually a parade was part of the celebration. Finally, in 1971, Columbus Day became a federal

This historical parade in Genoa, Italy, passes directly by the house of Christopher Columbus.

holiday. This means that on October 12 all government offices are closed. There is no mail delivery. Many businesses and schools do not open. It is supposed to be a day of celebration in honor of Christopher Columbus.

Revising Columbus Day

Not everyone celebrates Columbus Day. American Indians do not feel that Columbus was a hero. They dislike the cruel treatment

Many people, such as American Indians, do not believe Columbus Day should be celebrated.

their people received from Columbus and his men. In some cities American Indians have protested Columbus Day. They want to replace it with a different holiday that honors all Americans.

This new holiday is already celebrated in many Latin American countries. On October 12 those countries celebrate *Día de la Raza* (Day of the Race). This is a celebration of all people and of Columbus's voyages. There are usually parades, festivals, and speeches. In some cities in the United States things are changing, too. "Ethnic Diversity Day" has taken the place of Columbus Day activities in some areas.

How Do You Celebrate?

Today, Columbus Day is celebrated in different ways. Some of them have nothing to do with Columbus himself. Most towns and cities have parades. Some places do more.

Just Some Examples

Farmingdale, Long Island, in New York, has an annual Columbus Weekend Fair. This includes a carnival, barbecue, and live music. Stores have sidewalk sales. There is a magic show for children, and the event ends with fireworks.

Columbus Day is fun on Jack Frost Mountain in Pennsylvania. There is an arts and crafts festival. Over seventy artists take part. You can ride a chairlift up the mountain. And there is always lots of good food. The city of Columbus,

Kansas, celebrates in a big way. It hosts a fun-filled three-day festival. There is a Miss Columbus pageant and a classic car show. People go for hot-air balloon rides.

Some groups in Berkeley, California, celebrate in a different way. They enjoy Indigenous People's Day. This is a celebration of American Indian cultures. There are American Indian dances, foods, and crafts. The city of Columbus, Ohio, has been true to its name. It built a model of the *Santa María*. Actors there play the parts of the people from the voyage. Visitors can meet the actors and see the inner workings of the ship. They can hear how cannon fire signaled the *Niña* or *Pinta*. It is the next best thing to sailing with Columbus.

A Party in the Sky

In the city of Columbus, Kansas, Columbus Day is celebrated with a three-day festival. People go for hot-air balloon rides.

A Celebration of Exploration

Columbus Day is a good time to think about the past. But it is a good time to think about the future as well. Much has changed through the years. Today there are new frontiers to explore.

A replica of the *Santa María* sits docked in Columbus, Ohio.

In the fifteenth century, people explored the sea and the land. Now we are exploring space. Would Columbus have wanted to visit Mars? Would he have come up with a shorter route to get there? Whole new universes await us. Perhaps *you* will be among those who help explore them.

Columbus Day Craft*

Here are the supplies you will need:

Christopher Columbus liked to sail. This project will show you how to make your own small boat.

a 3-inch (7-centimeter) square of paper
crayons or markers
a toothpick
a small piece of colored clay
a large bottle cap

Directions:

1. Decorate the paper square with the crayons or markers. Make it as colorful as you like. It will be the boat's sail.

2. With a toothpick, poke one hole at the top and one hole at the bottom of the paper. Push the toothpick through one hole and out the other.

3. Roll the colored clay into a ball. Place it firmly in the middle of the inside of the large bottle cap.

4. Stick the end of the toothpick in the colored clay. The sail should stand up straight. Now your boat is ready to float in the sink or in a bowl of water.

Sailboat

Safety note: Be sure to ask for help from an adult, if needed, to complete this project.

Glossary

anniversary—The day each year when a past event is celebrated.

continent—One of the seven large land areas on the earth.

explorer—A person who travels to unknown places.

hardship—Something that causes great pain or suffering.

indigenous—Describes people who are native to a particular area.

monument—A building, statue, or plaque that honors a particular person or event.

native—A person who was born in the country in which he or she lives.

New World—The name sometimes used for North America and South America.

vessel—A ship or large boat.

voyage—A trip by water or through space.

Learn More

Books

Carr, Aaron. *Columbus Day.* New York, NY: AV2 by Weigl, 2015.

Dash, Meredith. *Columbus Day.* Minneapolis, MN: ABDO Kids, 2015.

Dayton, Connor. *Columbus Day.* New York, NY: PowerKids Press, 2012.

DeRubertis, Barbara, and Thomas Sperling. *Let's Celebrate Columbus Day.* New York, NY: The Kane Press, 2014.

Websites

AHC Arts & Crafts: Columbus Day Crafts for Kids
www.artistshelpingchildren.org/columbusdayartscraftsideasprojectskids.html
Get creative with these Columbus Day crafts!

DLTK's Columbus Day Activities for Kids
www.dltk-kids.com/crafts/columbus
Make more fun crafts for Columbus Day!

Enchanted Learning: Columbus Day Crafts and Activities
www.enchantedlearning.com/crafts/columbus/
Create crafts, write poems, and solve puzzles at this site devoted to Columbus Day activities.

Index

A
Africa, 8–10
American Indians, 7, 17–19, 23–24, 26
Asia, 7, 9–10, 12–13, 16, 18–19
Atlantic Ocean, 5, 7

C
Colombo, Christoforo; *See also* Columbus, Christopher
Colón, Cristobal; *See also* Columbus, Christopher
Columbus, Bartholomew (brother), 8–9
Columbus, Christopher
  birth, 8
  childhood, 8–9
  death, 19
  holiday celebrations, 5, 7, 21–24, 25–27
  marriage, 9
  official holiday declared, 22–23
  reaching land, 7, 16, 17–19
  returning to Spain, 19
  ships, 15–16, 19, 26
  voyage to "Asia," 5, 7, 9–10, 12, 13–14, 16, 18–19
  voyages to the New World, 5, 7, 17, 19, 21
  ways to honor, 21–24, 25–27
  young adulthood, 8–9
Columbus, Diego
  (brother), 8
  (son), 9, 13

D
Día de la Raza (Day of the Race), 24

E
East Indies, 17
Ethnic Diversity Day, 24
Europe/Europeans, 5, 7–8, 10, 12, 18

F
Ferdinand, King, 13–14, 19

G
Genoa, Italy, 5, 8

H
Harrison, Benjamin, 22

I
Indigenous People's Day, 26
Isabella, Queen, 13–14, 19

J
John II, King, 13

M
Moñiz, Felipa Perestrello de (wife), 9, 13

N
New World, 5, 7, 17, 19, 21
Niña, 15–16, 19, 26

P
Pinta, 15–16, 19, 26
pirates, 10
Portugal, 9, 13

S
Santa María, 15–16, 19, 26
Santangel, Luís de, 14–15
Spain, 13–16, 18–19

V
Vespucci, Amerigo, 21
Viking adventurers, 7

W
West Indies, 6–7, 17